Slow-down

Therapy

Slow~down Therapy

written by
Linus Mundy

illustrated by
R.W. Alley

ONE
CARING
PLACE
Abbey Press

Text © 1990 Linus Mundy
Illustrations © 1990 St. Meinrad Archabbey
Published by One Caring Place
Abbey Press
St. Meinrad, Indiana 47577

Library of Congress Catalog Number
90-81236

ISBN 0-87029-229-3

Printed in the United States of America

Foreword

In a hurry? Of course you are. Here in the Western world, we put a high value on efficiency, action, speed—and *results*. "Those who do, do. And those who don't? They sometimes get trampled."

It doesn't have to be that way. We can beat the system before it beats us to a frazzle.

Slow-down Therapy is not "Thirty-five Steps to Becoming Mostly Mellow." Rather, what you will find are thirty-five concrete ideas for helping you rediscover something you already possess: time, enough time. Here you will find tips for discovering your own ways to a more peaceful, relaxed use of time. These ways are there for the finding, even in the busiest life.

Turning these pages slowly can assist you in a rediscovery of the priceless prize of time, the priceless prize called life.

1.

Slow down; God is still in heaven. You are <u>not</u> responsible for doing it all—yourself—right now.

2.

Remember a happy, peaceful time in your past. Rest there. Each moment has a richness that takes a lifetime to savor.

3.

Set your own pace. When someone is pushing you, it's OK to tell them they're pushing.

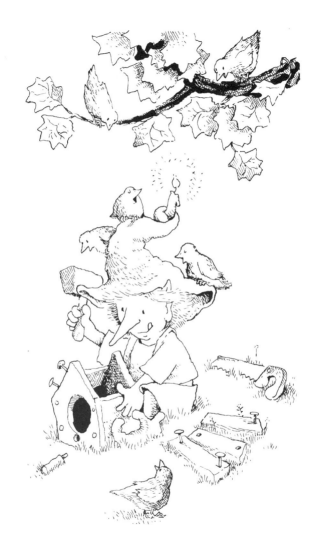

4.

Take nothing for granted:
watch water flow, the corn
grow, the leaves blow, your
neighbor mow.

5.

Taste your food. God gives it to delight as well as to nourish.

6.

Notice the sun and the moon as they rise and set. They are remarkable for their steady pattern of movement, not their speed.

7.

Quit planning how you're going
to <u>use</u> what you know, learn,
or possess. God's gifts just <u>are</u>;
be grateful and their purpose
will be clear.

8.

When you talk with someone, don't think about what you'll say next. Thoughts will spring up naturally if you let them.

9.

Talk and play with children.
It will bring out the unhurried
little person inside you.

10.

Create a place in your home...
at your work...in your heart...
where you can go for quiet and
recollection. You deserve it.

11.

Allow yourself time to be lazy and unproductive. Rest isn't a luxury; it's a necessity.

12.

Listen to the wind blow. It
carries a message of yesterday
and tomorrow—and now.
<u>Now</u> counts.

13.

Rest on your laurels. They bring comfort whatever their size, age, or condition.

14.

Talk slower. Talk less. Don't talk. Communication isn't measured by words.

15.

Give yourself permission to be late sometimes. Life is for living, not scheduling.

16.

Listen to the song of a bird—
the complete song. Music and
nature are gifts, but only if you
are willing to receive them.

17.

Take time just <u>to think</u>. Action is good and necessary, but it's fruitful only if we muse, ponder, and mull.

18.

Make time for play—the things <u>you</u> like to do. Whatever your age, your inner child needs re-creation.

19.

Watch and listen to the night sky. It speaks.

20.

Listen to the words you
speak—especially in prayer.

21.

Learn to stand back and let others take their turn as leaders. There will always be new opportunities for you to step out in front again.

22.

Divide big jobs into little jobs. If God took six days to create the universe, can you do any better?

23.

When you find yourself rushing
and anxious, stop. Ask yourself
<u>why</u> you are rushing and
anxious. The reasons may
improve your self-understanding.

24.

Take time to read—the Bible,
poetry, great books. Thoughtful
reading is enriching reading.

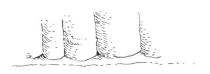

25.

Direct your life with purposeful choices, not with speed and efficiency. The best musician is one who plays with expression and meaning, not the one who finishes first.

26.

Take a day off alone; make a retreat. You can learn from monks and hermits without becoming one.

27.

Pet a furry friend. You will give
and get the gift of now.

28.

Work with your hands.
It frees the mind.

29.

Take time to wonder. Without wonder, life is merely existence.

30.

Sit in the dark. It will
teach you to see and hear,
taste and smell.

31.

Once in a while, turn down the lights, the volume, the throttle, the invitations. Less really can be more.

32.

Let go. Nothing is usually
the hardest thing to do —
but often it is the best.

33.

Take a walk—but don't go anywhere. If you walk just to get somewhere, you sacrifice the walking.

34.

When things are in chaos and
you are in a frenzy, ask yourself:
"What is <u>right</u> about now?"
Chances are, you already know
what is wrong.

35.

Count your blessings —
one at a time and slowly.

Linus Mundy is director of One Caring Place/ Publications at Abbey Press. He is also the author of *Keep-life-simple Therapy* and *Prayer-Walking*, and is a contributor to *Grief Therapy*. He lives with his wife and three children in Santa Claus, Indiana.

Illustrator for the Abbey Press Elf-help Books, **R.W. Alley** also illustrates and writes children's books. He lives in Barrington, Rhode Island, with his wife, daughter, and son.

The Story of the Abbey Press Elves

The engaging figures that populate the Abbey Press "elf-help" line of publications and products first appeared in 1987 on the pages of a small self-help book called *Be-good-to-yourself Therapy*. Shaped by the publishing staff's vision and defined in R.W. Alley's inventive illustrations, they lived out author Cherry Hartman's gentle, self-nurturing advice with charm, poignancy, and humor.

Reader response was so enthusiastic that more Elf-help Books were soon under way, a still-growing series that has inspired a line of related gift products.

The especially endearing character featured in the early books—sporting a cap with a mood-changing candle in its peak—has since been joined by a spirited female elf with flowers in her hair.

These two exuberant, sensitive, resourceful, kindhearted, lovable sprites, along with their lively elfin community, reveal what's truly important as they offer messages of joy and wonder, playfulness and co-creation, wholeness and serenity, the miracle of life and the mystery of God's love.

With wisdom and whimsy, these little creatures with long noses demonstrate the elf-help way to a rich and fulfilling life.

Elf-help Books

...adding "a little character" and a lot
of help to self-help reading!

Trust-in-God Therapy
#20119 $4.95   ISBN 0-87029-322-2

Elf-help for Overcoming Depression
#20134 $4.95   ISBN 0-87029-315-X

New Baby Therapy
#20140 $4.95   ISBN 0-87029-307-9

Grief Therapy for Men
#20141 $4.95   ISBN 0-87029-306-0

Living From Your Soul
#20146 $4.95   ISBN 0-87029-303-6

Teacher Therapy
#20145 $4.95   ISBN 0-87029-302-8

Be-good-to-your-family Therapy
#20154 $4.95   ISBN 0-87029-300-1

Stress Therapy
#20153 $4.95   ISBN 0-87029-301-X

Making-sense-out-of-suffering Therapy
#20156 $4.95   ISBN 0-87029-296-X

Get Well Therapy
#20157 $4.95   ISBN 0-87029-297-8

Anger Therapy
#20127 $4.95   ISBN 0-87029-292-7

Caregiver Therapy
#20164 $4.95   ISBN 0-87029-285-4

Self-esteem Therapy
#20165 $4.95   ISBN 0-87029-280-3

Take-charge-of-your-life Therapy
#20168 $4.95   ISBN 0-87029-271-4

Work Therapy
#20166 $4.95   ISBN 0-87029-276-5

Everyday-courage Therapy
#20167 $4.95   ISBN 0-87029-274-9

Peace Therapy
#20176 $4.95   ISBN 0-87029-273-0

Friendship Therapy
#20174 $4.95   ISBN 0-87029-270-6

Christmas Therapy (color edition)
#20175 $5.95   ISBN 0-87029-268-4

Grief Therapy
#20178 $4.95   ISBN 0-87029-267-6

More Be-good-to-yourself Therapy
#20180 $3.95   ISBN 0-87029-262-5

Happy Birthday Therapy
#20181 $4.95   ISBN 0-87029-260-9

Forgiveness Therapy
#20184 $4.95   ISBN 0-87029-258-7

Keep-life-simple Therapy
#20185 $4.95   ISBN 0-87029-257-9

Be-good-to-your-body Therapy
#20188 $4.95   ISBN 0-87029-255-2

Celebrate-your-womanhood Therapy
#20189 $4.95   ISBN 0-87029-254-4